D1417441

ARLEIGH BURKE DESTROYERS

BY CARLOS ALVAREZ

BELLWETHER MEDIA · MINNEAPOLIS, MN

Are you ready to take it to the extreme?
Torque books thrust you into the action-packed
world of sports, vehicles, and adventure. These books
may include dirt, smoke, fire, and dangerous stunts.
WARNING: read at your own risk.

Library of Congress Cataloging-in-Publication Data

Alvarez, Carlos, 1968-
  Arleigh Burke destroyers / by Carlos Alvarez.
       p. cm. – (Torque: military machines)
  Includes bibliographical references and index.
  Summary: "Amazing photography accompanies engaging information about Arleigh Burke
destroyers. The combination of high-interest subject matter and light text is intended for students
in grades 3 through 7"–Provided by publisher.
  ISBN 978-1-60014-331-1 (hardcover : alk. paper)
  1. Guided missile ships–Juvenile literature. 2. Destroyers (Warships)–United States–Juvenile
literature. I. Title.
  V825.3.A75 2010
  623.825'4–dc22
                                                          2009037596

The images in this book are reproduced through the courtesy of: Ted Carlson / Fotodynamics, cover;
all other photos courtesy of the Department of Defense.

Printed in the United States of America, North Mankato, MN.
010110   1149

CONTENTS

THE ARLEIGH BURKE DESTROYER IN ACTION

A United States Navy **aircraft carrier** floats off an enemy shore. Planes take off from the carrier to bomb targets on land. The enemy launches an attack on the aircraft carrier. The aircraft carrier is not alone. An Arleigh Burke destroyer sailing next to the carrier is ready for the attack.

Some Arleigh Burke destroyers carry helicopters.
Helicopters can be used to scout, as rescue craft,
and in battle.

The destroyer crew quickly responds. Powerful guided missiles streak into the sky. They slam into enemy aircraft. Crew members load and fire **torpedoes** at enemy ships. The enemy is quickly losing aircraft and ships. The enemy retreats. The Arleigh Burke destroyer has protected the **fleet**.

★ **FAST FACT** ★

The earliest destroyers were called *torpedo boat destroyers*.
Their main job was to battle small torpedo boats.

GUIDED-MISSILE DESTROYER

Arleigh Burke destroyers protect other warships in a fleet. They are armed with torpedoes, guns, guided missiles, and other weapons. The destroyers are small and light. This makes them fast and easy to maneuver.

The U.S. Navy built the first Arleigh Burke destroyers in 1991. They replaced the Spruance class. The new class was named for Admiral Arleigh Burke. Burke was a U.S. Navy destroyer captain during World War II and the Korean War.

Admiral Arleigh Burke

WEAPONS AND FEATURES

Arleigh Burke destroyers use the powerful **Aegis Combat System (ACS)**. It helps the crew detect threats, choose targets, and fire missiles. Tomahawk cruise missiles have advanced guidance systems. They can lock on to a target and change direction while in flight.

Tomahawk cruise missile

Arleigh Burke destroyers use surface-to-air missiles to take down enemy aircraft.

Arleigh Burke destroyers have many other weapons as well. An MK 45 gun shoots powerful rounds. Two torpedo launchers can target surface ships. **Depth charges** explode deep underwater. Destroyers use them to attack **submarines**.

Torpedo launcher

MK 45

ARLEIGH BURKE DESTROYER
SPECIFICATIONS:

Primary Function: Guided-missile destroyer

Length: 509.5 feet (155 meters)

Beam (Width): 59 feet (18 meters)

Displacement (Weight): 9,200 tons (8,350 metric tons)

Top Speed: 36 miles (57 kilometers) per hour

Engines: 4 General Electric LM 2500-30 gas turbines

Arleigh Burke destroyers are **durable**. They have solid steel frames. Many earlier destroyers had frames that included lightweight aluminum. The steel frame makes the Arleigh Burke destroyer stronger than earlier destroyers.

ARLEIGH BURKE
MISSIONS

The main **mission** for destroyers is to **escort** and protect other ships. They usually travel in **carrier battle groups**. These groups of warships surround huge aircraft carriers. Aircraft carriers are big, slow targets. They need other ships to defend them.

A destroyer needs a large crew. An Arleigh Burke destroyer has between 276 and 380 crew members. The captain is in charge of the ship. Other officers help the captain run the ship. Enlisted members operate the weapons systems and maintain the engines. They also clean the ship and do many other duties. The crew works together to keep the fleet safe from harm.

GLOSSARY

Aegis Combat System (ACS)—an advanced computer system that links a ship's sensors and weapons together

aircraft carrier—a huge Navy ship from which airplanes can take off and land; an aircraft carrier is like a floating airport.

carrier battle group—a small group of warships that travel together, based around an aircraft carrier

depth charge—a device dropped off of a destroyer that explodes underwater; destroyers use depth charges to target submarines.

durable—long-lasting and tough

escort—to travel with and protect another person or vehicle

fleet—a large group of warships

mission—a military task

submarine—a warship that is able to travel underwater

torpedo—an explosive that travels underwater

TO LEARN MORE

AT THE LIBRARY

David, Jack. *The United States Navy*. Minneapolis, Minn.: Bellwether Media, 2008.

Green, Michael. *Destroyers: The Arleigh Burke Class*. Mankato, Minn.: Capstone Press, 2005.

Zobel, Derek. *Nimitz Aircraft Carriers*. Minneapolis, Minn.: Bellwether Media, 2009.

ON THE WEB

Learning more about military machines is as easy as 1, 2, 3.

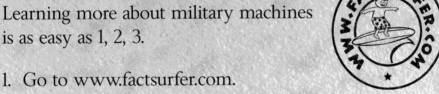

1. Go to www.factsurfer.com.

2. Enter "military machines" into the search box.

3. Click the "Surf" button and you will see a list of related Web sites.

With factsurfer.com, finding more information is just a click away.

INDEX